EVERY
MAN GOTTA RIGHT
TO DECIDE HIS OWN
DESTINY.

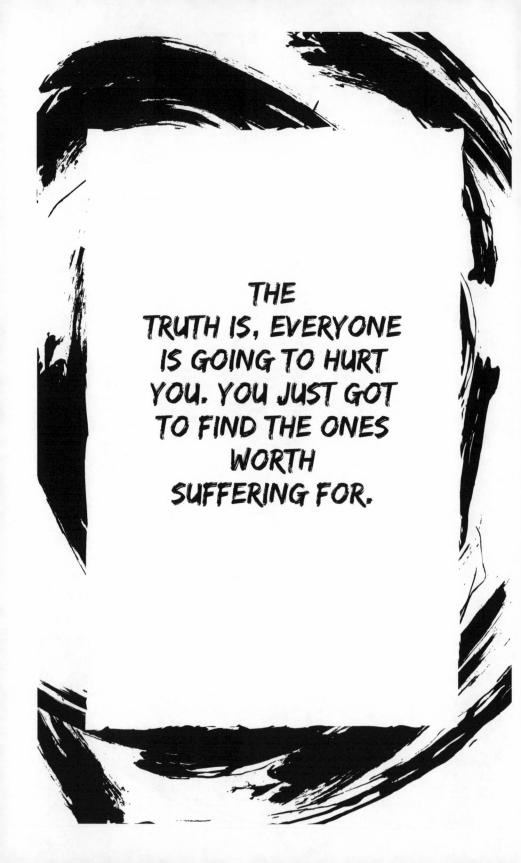

I DON'T
BELIEVE IN DEATH,
NEITHER IN FLESH
NOR IN SPIRIT.

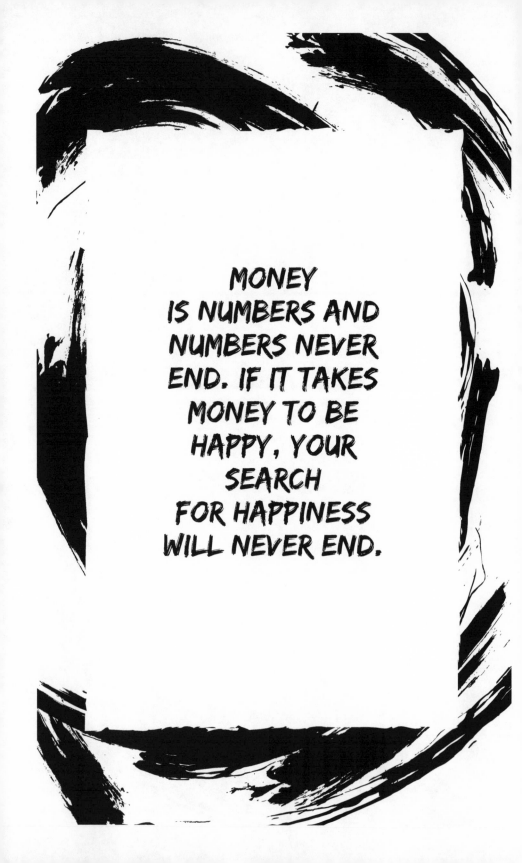

MONEY
IS NUMBERS AND
NUMBERS NEVER
END. IF IT TAKES
MONEY TO BE
HAPPY, YOUR
SEARCH
FOR HAPPINESS
WILL NEVER END.

WHEN YOU
SMOKE THE HERB,
IT REVEALS YOU TO
YOURSELF.

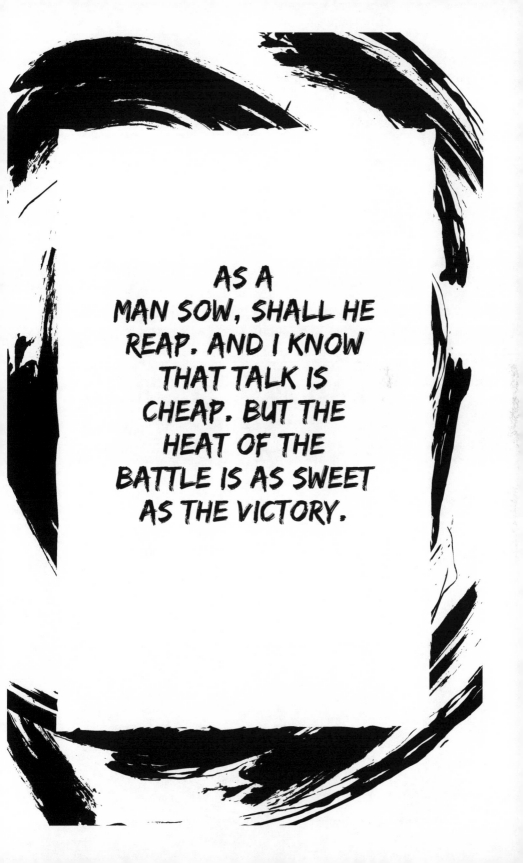

AS A
MAN SOW, SHALL HE
REAP. AND I KNOW
THAT TALK IS
CHEAP. BUT THE
HEAT OF THE
BATTLE IS AS SWEET
AS THE VICTORY.

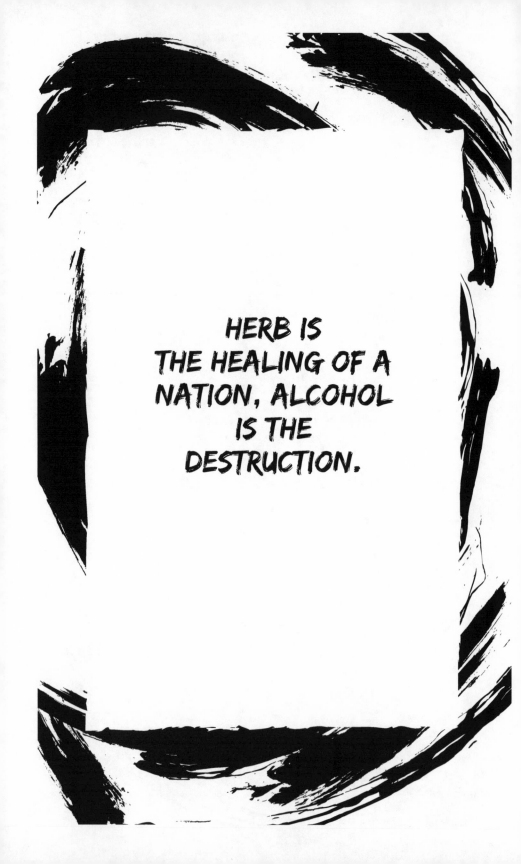

IN LIFE,
I KNOW THERE IS A
LOT OF GRIEF BUT
YOUR LOVE IS MY
RELIEF.

MAN IS
A UNIVERSE WITHIN
HIMSELF.

ONE GOOD
THING ABOUT
MUSIC, WHEN IT HITS
YOU, YOU FEEL NO
PAIN.

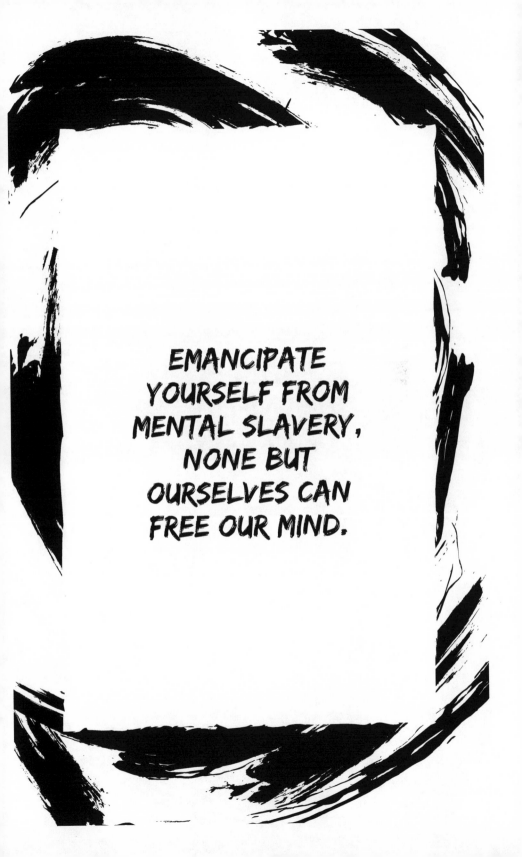

EMANCIPATE
YOURSELF FROM
MENTAL SLAVERY,
NONE BUT
OURSELVES CAN
FREE OUR MIND.

THE
POWER OF
PHILOSOPHY FLOATS
THROUGH MY HEAD..
LIGHT LIKE A
FEATHER, HEAVY AS
LEAD.

ONLY
ONCE IN YOUR LIFE,
I TRULY BELIEVE,
YOU FIND SOMEONE
WHO CAN
COMPLETELY TURN
YOUR WORLD
AROUND.

GOD SENT
ME ON EARTH. HE
SEND ME TO DO
SOMETHING, AND
NOBODY CAN STOP
ME. IF GOD WANT
TO STOP ME, THEN I
STOP. MAN NEVER
CAN.

THE DAY
YOU STOP RACING
IS THE DAY YOU WIN
THE RACE.

EVERYTHING
IS POLITICAL. I WILL
NEVER BE A
POLITICIAN OR EVEN
THINK POLITICAL.
ME JUST
DEAL WITH LIFE AND
NATURE. THAT IS
THE GREATEST
THING TO ME.

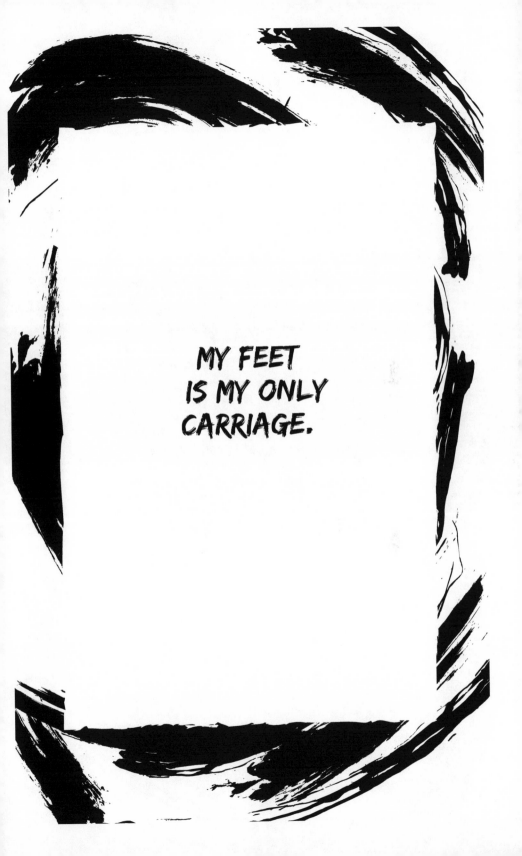

YOU
ENTERTAIN PEOPLE
WHO ARE SATISFIED.
HUNGRY PEOPLE
CAN'T BE
ENTERTAINED   OR
PEOPLE WHO ARE
AFRAID. YOU CAN'T
ENTERTAIN A MAN
WHO HAS NO FOOD.

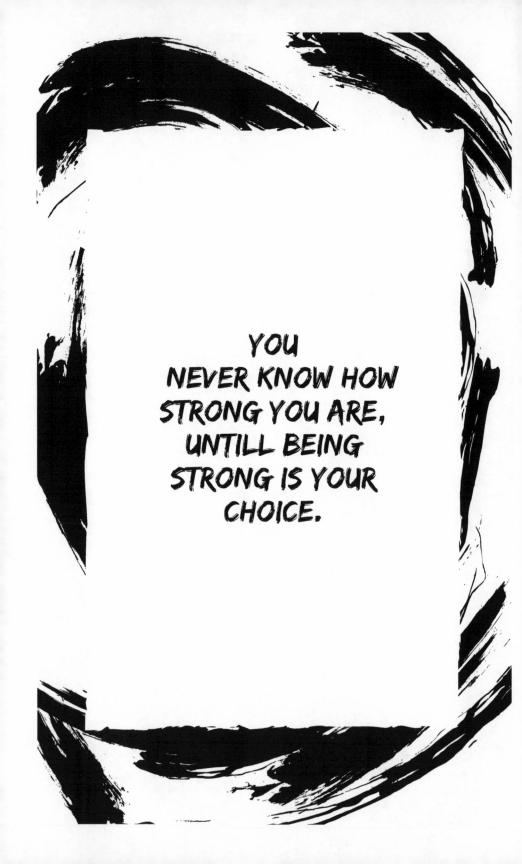

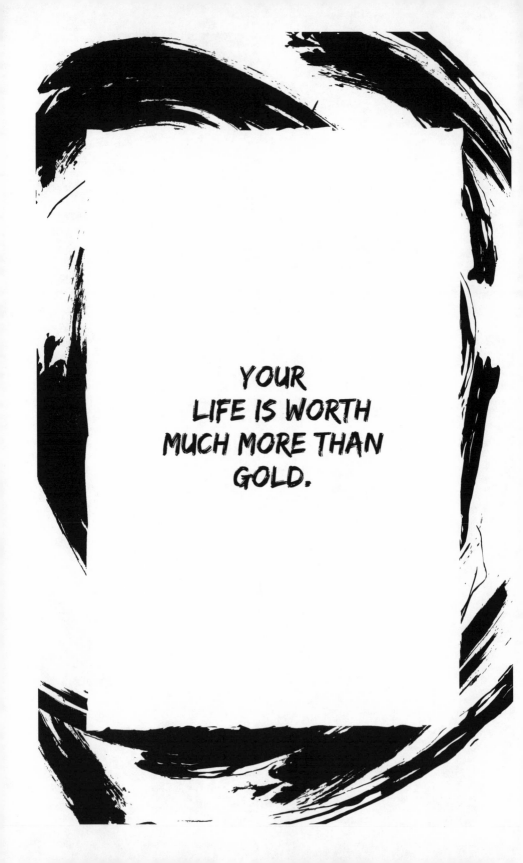

YOUR
LIFE IS WORTH
MUCH MORE THAN
GOLD.

THE MORE
PEOPLE SMOKE
HERB, THE MORE
BABYLON FALL.

WHAT
IMPORTANT IS MAN
SHOULD LIVE IN
RIGHTEOUSNESS,
IN NATURAL LOVE
FOR
MANKIND.

DON'T
BURY YOUR
THOUGHTS, PUT
YOUR VISION TO
REALITY.

TRIED TO
RUN AWAY, BUT
THE ROAD LEADS
BACK TO YOU.

THE
BIGGEST COWARD
OF A MAN IS TO
AWAKEN THE LOVE
OF A WOMEN
WITHOUT THE
INTENSION OF
LOVING HER.

WHEN ONE
DOOR IS CLOSED,
DON'T YOU KNOW,
ANOTHER IS OPEN.

IT IS
BETTER TO LIVE
ON THE HOUSE
TOP THAN TO
LIVE IN A HOUSE
FULL OF
CONFUSION.

ONE
LOVE, ONE
HEART.

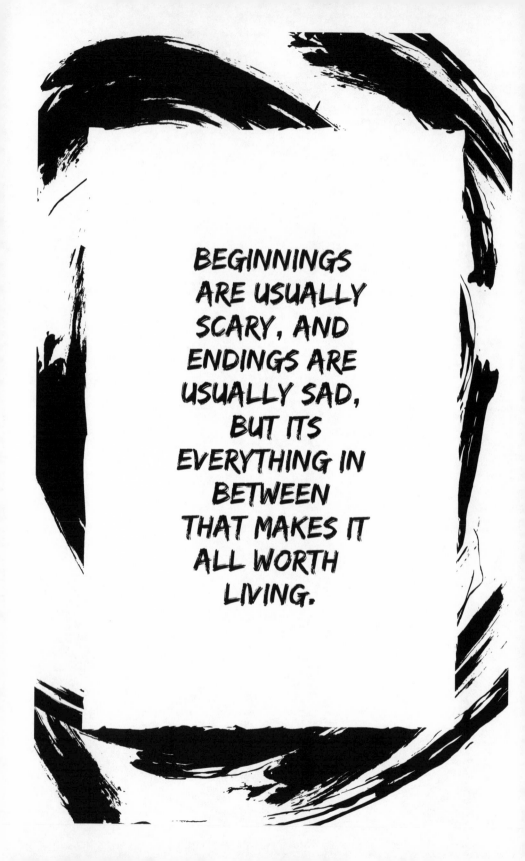

THE
STONE THAT THE
BUILDER REFUSED
SHALL BE THE
HEAD CORNER
STONE.

IT TAKE
MANY A YEAR,
MON, AND MAYBE
SOME BLOODSHED
MUST BE, BUT
RIGHTEOUSNESS
SOMEDAY
PREVAIL.

FREE
SPEECH CARRIES
WITH IT SOME
FREEDOM TO
LISTEN.

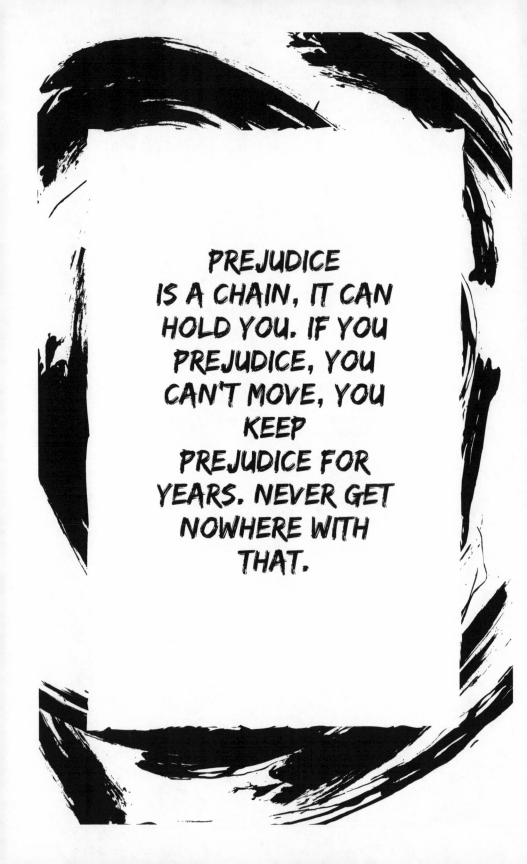

PREJUDICE
IS A CHAIN, IT CAN
HOLD YOU. IF YOU
PREJUDICE, YOU
CAN'T MOVE, YOU
KEEP
PREJUDICE FOR
YEARS. NEVER GET
NOWHERE WITH
THAT.

BOB
MARLEY ISN'T MY
NAME. I DON'T
EVEN KNOW MY
NAME YET.

THE GREATNESS OF
A MAN IS NOT IN
HOW MUCH WEALTH
HE ACQUIRES, BUT
IN HIS INTEGRITY
AND HIS ABILITY TO
AFFECT THOSE
AROUND HIM
POSITIVELY.

WHEN
THE ROOT IS
STRONG, THE FRUIT
IS SWEET.

LIVE FOR YOURSELF
AND YOU WILL LIVE
IN VAIN LIVE FOR
OTHERS, AND YOU
WILL LIVE AGAIN.

THE
WINDS THAT
SOMETIMES TAKE
SOMETHING WE
LOVE, ARE THE
SAME THAT BRING
US
SOMETHING WE
LEARN TO LOVE.

MY FEAR
IS MY ONLY
COURAGE.

JUST
BECAUSE YOU ARE
HAPPY IT DOES
NOT MEAN THAT THE
DAY IS PERFECT
BUT THAT YOU
HAVE LOOKED
BEYOND ITS
IMPERFECTIONS.

WHAT YOU
IS IS WHAT YOU IS.
FROM BEGINNING
TO THE END.

I NO
HAVE EDUCATION.
I HAVE INSPIRATION.
IF I WAS EDUCATED
I WOULD BE A
DAMN
FOOL.

ROAD OF
LIFE IS ROCKY
AND YOU MAY
STUMBLE TOO, SO
WHILE
YOU TALK ABOUT
ME,
SOMEONE ELSE IS
JUDGING YOU.

18375547R00063